THE •FANCY •DRESS
PARTY
BOOK

MARIA GORDON

HAMLYN

PARTY TIPS AND HINTS

Make this book the beginning of some fantastic fancy dress parties. Take its ideas and turn them into your own incredible inventions. You can try fabric instead of paper, tape instead of glue or you could change the colours and swap around the games. Try experimenting with props and dream up lots more unusual costumes and funny food ideas.

This book is just a start. See if your imagination can take you even further!

ACKNOWLEDGEMENTS

Costumes and props made by Karen Radford
and Maria Gordon
Make-up artist – Jacqueline Russon
Party food made by Ann Marie Mulligan
and Maria Gordon
Photographs by David Johnson
Illustrations by Peter Bull
Cartoons by Mike Gordon

HAMLYN CHILDREN'S BOOKS

Editor: Anne Civardi
Designer: Mark Summersby
Production Controller: Ruth Charlton

Published in 1993 by
Hamlyn Children's Books
Part of Reed International Books,
Michelin House, 81 Fulham Road, London SW3 6RB
and Auckland, Melbourne, Singapore and Toronto.

This paperback edition first published in 1994

ISBN 0 600 58367 8

British Library Catologuing-in-Publication Data
A catalogue record for this book is available from the British Library

Books printed and bound in Italy

The author would like to thank Anne and Mike and all the lovely children photographed in the book.

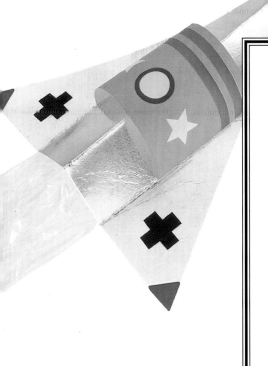

CONTENTS

PERFECT PARTIES

When is your next party and what kind of party would you like it to be? This book is packed with lots of crazy ideas for fancy dress parties to choose from. There's a spooky party, a weird alien party and a really royal kings and queens party.

Or choose from a wild jungle party, a flashy pop star party and a pirate party. Decide which one you'd like best and then start planning. Some are a bit more work than others, but there is no sewing and not very much cooking.

INVITATIONS

Before you send out your invitations, decide where and how long your party should be. Would it be best outdoors, at home, in a hall or even at a park? How many people should you ask and who should they be?

Then start to work on the invitations ready to send them out two weeks before your party. Make sure you find out exactly who can come and who cannot so that you can make the right amount of food and buy enough presents for your guests to take home.

PAINTING FACES

Make yourself look even better by painting your face to match your costume. Water-based paints are much better than cream or grease sticks. Use them with sable or oxhair brushes and small sponges.

Put on the background and lighter colours first. For deeper colours use a second or third coat. Theatrical glitter gel gives a really special effect.

CHOOSING COSTUMES

Ask your mum or dad to help you choose the best party and which costumes, props and food to make. Many of the ideas can be changed slightly to suit different parties. You can also create your own special costumes.

Before you start, collect all the things you need for your costume. You might need an adult to help with measuring to make sure it fits well. You can choose which colours you want it to be. The ideas in the book are just a guide.

DECORATIONS

Next you should make the decorations, party bags and anything you need for the party games. There are lots of things to make that give your party the right atmosphere, such as space scenes, jungle nets and royal banners.

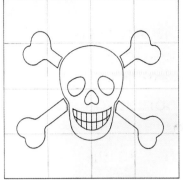

USING A GRID

To help you draw some of the shapes in the book, we have shown them on grids. This is how you use a grid.

1 Notice whether or not your paper or card should be folded in half and where the fold should come.

draw on squares 5cm x 5cm

2 Rule the squares on to the card with a pencil. For the grids in this book, make the sides of each square 5 cm long. A grid with four squares would then measure 20 cm x 20 cm.

copy shape you need on to grid

3 Copy the shape you want on to the grid. Notice where the lines of the drawing cross the lines of the grid and draw it bit by bit.

cut out shape

4 When the drawing is finished cut it out. Rub out the grid lines and use the shape you have cut out.

FUN FOOD

Leave the food till last to make sure it is really fresh. But you will have to buy the ingredients in advance. Ask your mum or dad to tell you when it is the best time to make the food you have chosen and to help you prepare it. Some of the things might be fun for everyone to make at the party.

PARTY PLANS

It is a good idea to plan what you want to happen at your party and write it all down. Will you play games with your guests as soon as they arrive? Or would you prefer to make things? When will you all eat? When is the best time to open your presents?

When the big day arrives, make sure everything is absolutely ready. Hang up the decorations, set out the party table, fill the party bags, dress up and be ready to greet your friends.

Then there is one last thing you must not forget. It is very, very important - HAVE A GREAT PARTY WHICH IS LOTS OF FUN!

PIRATE PARTY

Turn your house or garden into a pirate's den decorated with lots of Jolly Roger flags, chests full of sparkling treasure and some crazy colourful parrots. Ask your guests to dress up as cruel captains or sneaky smugglers. When they arrive send them on a hunt for pirate's swag before you treat them to some delicious treasure island food.

ISLAND INVITATIONS

yellow island shape

20cm

20cm

1 Cut out a square of blue paper, 20 cm x 20 cm, for each guest. This is the sea. Cut out and glue a yellow island shape on to each blue square.

2 Glue round, green patches on each island, and a tall palm tree shape. Add shark fins and crosses to turn your invitations into treasure island maps.

ANNA

3 Write all your party details in a trail around the islands. Then roll up the invitations and tie them up with string to give or send to your guests.

SMUGGLER'S TIPS

Ask an adult to burn the end of a cork. Use the burnt end to paint curly pirate moustaches on you and your mates.

Make a pirate captain's golden hoop earrings from two brass curtain rings. Thread a length of cotton through each ring and tie it in a loop around each ear. The curtain rings will dangle down just like real pirate's earrings.

CAPTAIN'S HAT

Things you need:
Stiff red paper
Strip of black crêpe paper,
8 cm wide and 75 cm long
Sticky-backed plastic
Scissors, glue, sticky tape
and a stapler

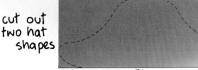

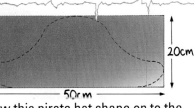

cut out two hat shapes

20cm

50cm

1 Draw this pirate hat shape on to the red paper folded in half (see page 5 for grid). Cut it out, making two hat shapes. One is the back, the other the front.

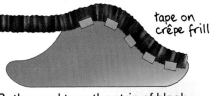

tape on crêpe frill

2 Gather and tape the strip of black crêpe paper to the front hat shape, like this, leaving about 6 cm showing above the top of the hat.

stick on jolly roger shape

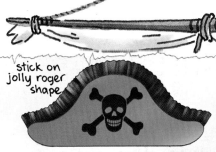

3 Cut out a Jolly Roger shape from the black sticky-backed plastic. Stick it on the front of your hat (see page 5).

staple sides together

4 Glue or staple the front and back hat shapes together, at the sides. Draw a coloured line around the edge.

SHARK SPOTTER

Things you need:
3 long cardboard tubes, such
as cardboard kitchen rolls
Black paper or black paint
A paintbrush
Gold or silver foil
Scissors, sticky tape and glue

cut off one third

cut in half

leave whole

1 Cut a third off one of the cardboard tubes and throw it away. Cut one of the other tubes in half. Throw one half away. Leave the third tube whole.

overlap and tape

3 Overlap and tape the medium tube so that it fits snugly inside the big one. Overlap and tape the small tube so it fits inside the medium tube, as shown.

gold or silver strips

4 Glue strips of gold or silver foil around both ends of the big tube and around one end of each of the other two tubes.

slit down length of tube

slit down length

2 Cut the medium-sized tube down its length. Do the same to the small tube. Then cover all three tubes with black paper or paint them black.

SMUGGLER'S RIG OUT

To look like a sneaky smuggler, wear a stripy T-shirt and a pair of cut-off jeans. Knot a bright scarf around your neck and one around your head. Add a belt, a sword and an eyepatch. Now you can start smuggling.

PIRATE PROPS

To give your pirate party a desert island feeling, hang up a big garden net. Cut out and paint lots of fishy shapes and fasten them on to the net. You could also hang up some fake jewellery to look like stolen treasure.

Turn your party table upside down to make it look like a real raft for all your pirate friends to eat around.

BALANCING PARROTS

Things you need:
Sheets of thin white card
A pencil, ruler and scissors
Felt tip pens, paints or crayons

draw parrot shape on grid

30cm

15cm

1 Ask an adult to help you draw this parrot shape on a sheet of thin card, using a grid (see page 5). You might like to draw lots of parrots in different sizes.

cut out parrot shape

2 Cut out the parrot and draw around it on to the other sheets of card. Draw one parrot for every guest and more to decorate the room. Cut them out.

3 Colour or paint the parrots brightly. Then balance them on their claws all around the room. If they don't balance well, fasten a paperclip to their tails.

TREASURE FOOD CHESTS

You will need a small shoe box for each guest. Slit the corners on one long edge of the lid. Hinge the lid by taping the edge along one side of the shoe box.

Paint the boxes different colours or cover them with coloured paper and decorate them with a gold felt tip pen. Then write on your guests' names. Glue a few gold coins to each box.

Line them with a red paper napkin and fill them with party food. At the end of the party, let your friends take their treasure chests home full of party loot.

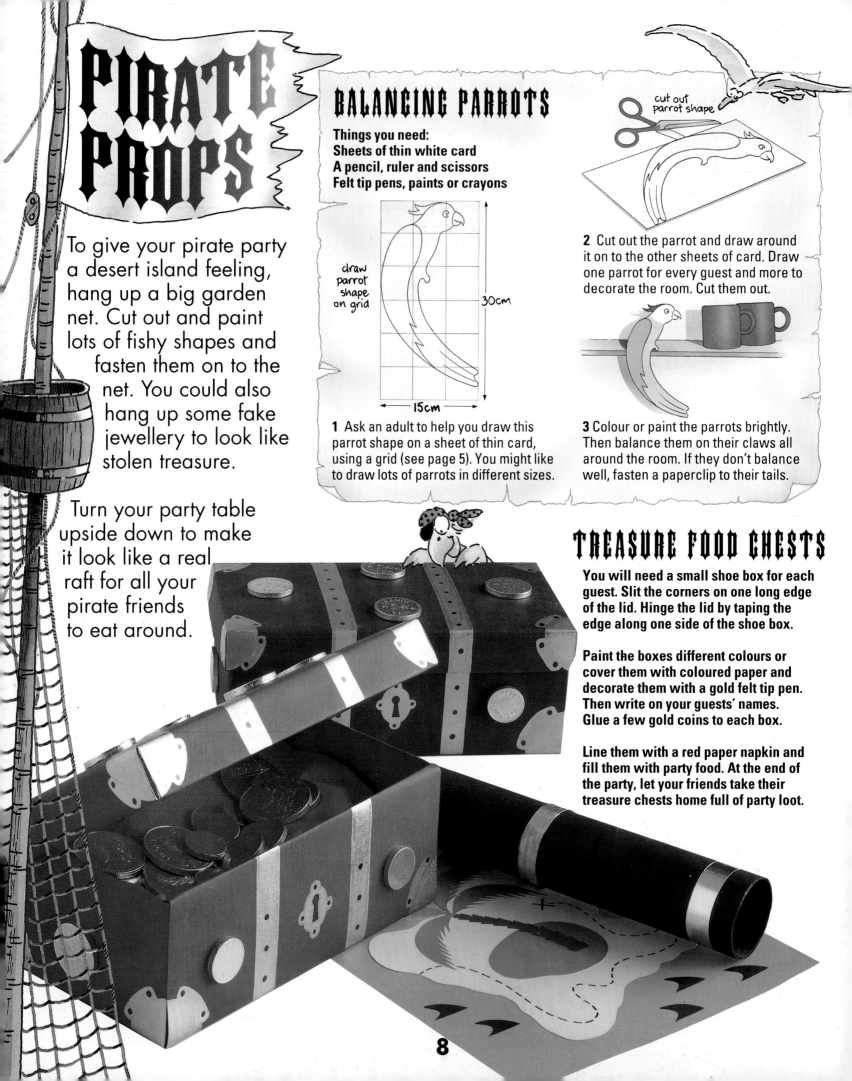

GALLEON GAMES

DEEP SEA MONSTERS

For this noisy game, you will need about 10 squeakers, the sort that go inside teddy bears. They are cheap to buy from fabric and craft shops.

Spread out a duvet on the floor. This is the sea. Scatter the squeakers under the sea. Then take it in turns to be blindfolded, spun around and led to the sea.

Everyone must try to walk right across the sea without treading on a squeaker. If they do, they have woken up a monster and are out. They are also out if they walk off the edge of the sea.

ARE YOU THERE, LONG JOHN?

Before the party starts, stuff the foot of one leg of a pair of tights with more tights, socks or soft fabric. Knot the other end tightly. Now you have made a soft smuggler's club for the game.

To play, two pirates lie down on their tummies, head to head, with their arms stretched out in front of them. They hold each other's left hand.

Both are blindfolded and one pirate is given the club in his free hand.

He shouts 'Are you there, Long John?' The other pirate replies, 'Yes', but then quickly tries to dodge before the other pirate swings the club and tries to hit him. Each pirate has three turns in a row. The first pirate to score six hits is the winner.

TREASURE HUNT

Ask an adult to lay a trail of clues, one for you and one for each guest, all around the house or garden. These can be either picture clues or word clues. Everyone follows them, taking it in turn to lead the way and read the clues. The last clue leads to a bag or chest filled with party surprises for everyone.

SMUGGLER'S DIP

Wrap up enough small party presents for every guest and bury them in a bucket full of sand or torn up paper shreds. Make the bucket look like a barrel by covering it with brown crêpe paper. Then wrap two or three bands of black crêpe paper round the bucket. Stand a big Jolly Roger flag in the sand.

As your guests leave, let them dip into the sand and find a buried party present to take home.

jolly roger flag

black crêpe paper

brown crêpe paper

TREASURE ISLAND FOOD

Hang coconuts and bananas from your smuggler's net. Pretend everyone is stranded round a table raft, then serve delicious treasure island cakes in a sea of blue jelly to your greedy pirates. Fill their treasure chests with tasty treats, like sausage rafts and fishy sandwiches.

COCONUT FROSTIES

Dip the rim of a long glass that has been cooled in the fridge, first in lemon juice, then in desiccated coconut. Pour in ice cold tropical fruit juice and decorate the frosted rim with a big round slice of orange or lemon.

SAUSAGE RAFTS

Make a raft by joining four cooked baby sausages together with a cocktail stick through each end. Cut a triangle from a slice of cheese to make a sail. Thin processed cheese slices are the best to use.

Push the sail on to another cocktail stick and stand it in the middle of the raft. Instead of using baby sausages you could make hot dog rafts.

FISHING NET FILLERS

Make sandwiches with sticky fillings, such as cream cheese or peanut butter. Then, using cookie or dough cutters, press out lots of fish shapes from the sandwiches.

Use food colouring to paint on scales, eyes and mouths. Then serve your fishy sandwiches in their own little nets.

TREASURE ISLANDS

Things you need:
Fairy cakes
50 g soft butter
115 g sifted icing sugar
½-1 tablespoon water
Green food colouring
Wafers and raisins
Hundreds and thousands

add icing sugar

1 Beat the butter until it is smooth. Then add the icing sugar bit by bit, beating the mixture well.

add green food colouring

2 Mix in a few drops of green food colouring to the icing. Add the water, a few drops at a time, until you have a thick, creamy icing.

green icing

wafer palm tree

3 Ask an adult to help you cut the wafers into palm tree shapes. Paint the tops of the trees and fairy cakes with the green icing.

stick on raisins

push tree into slit

jelly sea

4 Stick a raisin on the top of each tree. Sprinkle the cakes with hundreds and thousands and cut a slit in the top of each one. Place a tree in each slit and serve the cakes as treasure islands in the blue jelly sea. Stick sharks' fins cut from wafer chocolates into the jelly.

BLUE JELLY SEA

Make up a packet of lime jelly with a little less water than usual. Add enough drops of blue food colouring to turn it blue. Pour the jelly into a shallow glass serving dish. When it has set, chop it up roughly with a sharp knife.

Spooky party

A really spooky party is fun to give, especially at Hallowe'en. To make your house look extra scary, hang up lots of creepy decorations, like black balloons, spooky spiders and batty bats. Ask your ghostie guests to dress up as really wicked witches, swooping bats, moaning mummies, and skeletons or ghosts. Give them foul party food, like severed jelly hands, and play lots of grisly games.

Ghostie Invite

1 Cut out a rectangle of coloured paper for every guest. If you use black paper, you may need to write in gold or silver. Make a crease 2.5 cm from the edge. Fold the rest of the paper in half.

2 Cut out a ghost shape for every guest from a sheet of white paper. Draw on eyes and smiley mouths and then glue them on to the coloured paper rectangles, like this.

3 Write all the details of your party around the ghostie's tail. Make the bottom crease a reply slip. Then cut around the top of your ghost, so that it pops up when you stand the card up.

Witch's Hat

Things you need:
2 big sheets of thin card or thick paper
A big black rubbish bag and orange wool
Scissors, strong glue and sticky tape

45cm
60cm
32.5cm

1 Cut out this cone shape and hat brim from the card. Cut a big hole in the brim to fit your head. Open out the black bag. Cut out two circles, one the same size as the brim, the other just bigger.

2 Glue the bigger circle to one side of the brim. Cut tabs where it overlaps and glue them down. Poke a hole in the middle of the plastic with scissors. Cut tabs to the brim. Glue them down.

3 From the bag, cut a cone shape, about 2.5 cm bigger all around than your card cone. Cut off the top of the card cone. Stick the bag shape to the card cone, leaving the top free.

4 Cut tabs, 1.5 cm long, around the bottom of the cone shape. Curl the cardboard into a cone and fit it inside the brim. Tape the tabs underneath. Tape the side of your hat in place.

5 Stick the second black bag circle under the brim. Cut tabs from the middle and glue them inside your hat. Glue strands of orange wool inside the hat to make horrible straggly hair.

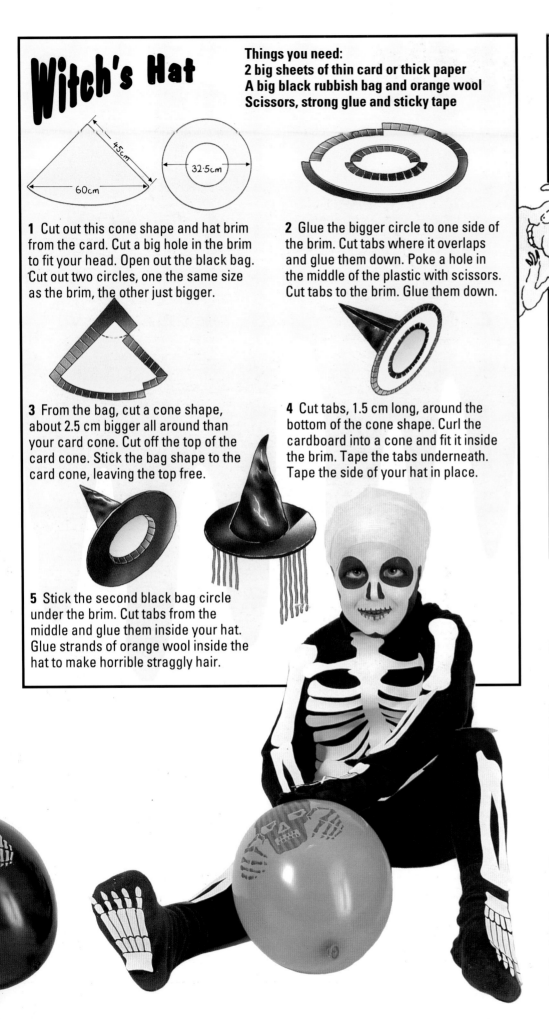

Creepy Cloak

Things you need:
A black rubbish bag or black fabric
Green ribbon, scissors and glue

30cm
75cm
105cm

1 Cut open a black rubbish bag and lay it on the floor. Draw this cloak shape on to the plastic with a felt pen or chalk. Cut out the shape.

2 Cut small slits along the top of the cloak and thread some green ribbon through them, as shown. Cut a fringe along the bottom of the cloak.

Spooky Tips

To make yourself look like a wicked witch, paint your face green and black. Wear a black T-shirt, black tights, black shoes, fingerless gloves and black nail varnish. Cut out spooky shapes and glue them on to your hat and cloak.

Scary Skeleton

Turn yourself into a scary skeleton by cutting out big bone shapes from white or green paper. Stick them on to a black T-shirt and tights, or trousers. It is best to use double-sided tape. Wear a white swimming cap for an eerie skull effect.

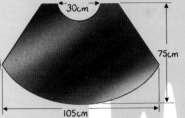

Spooky Spiders

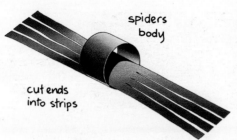

spiders body

cut ends into strips

Things you need:
Stiff black paper
Scissors
Sticky tape and glue
White paint and a black pen

2 Cut each end of the second strip into four legs, leaving 2.5 cm in the middle. Push the strip through the spider's body. Glue it in the middle.

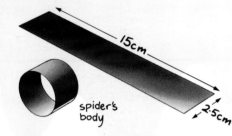

15cm

spider's body

2.5cm

curl legs

paint on eyes

1 Cut out two strips of black paper, 2.5 cm by 15 cm. Wind one of the strips loosely around your finger. Tape the end down firmly. This is the spider's body.

3 Paint two big spooky white or yellow eyes on the body. Then curl the legs down by dragging them between your first finger and thumb nails.

Witchy Pets

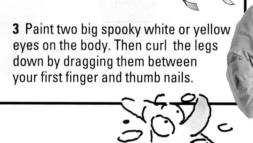

Thread a needle with a long piece of strong thread. Tie a knot in the end. Push the needle through a spooky spider and then the brim of the witch's hat.

Push the needle through the floppy plastic at the top, down through the brim on the other side and through another spooky spider. Knot the loose end. Now pull one spider down and watch the other zoom up to the brim.

Moaning Mummy

To make yourself into a moaning mummy, ask someone to wrap you all over in lavatory paper while you keep your arms and legs slightly bent. Wear white face paint, with a splash of red paint for blood, white tights and T-shirt.

Work around and around, criss-crossing the paper from your waist down each leg, taping it down as you go. Wrap your top half separately, criss-crossing over the shoulders, then around the arms and hands. Do your head and neck last of all.

Bat Wings

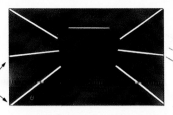

cardboard strips

tape over strip

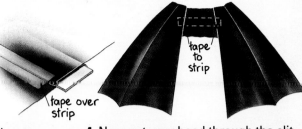

tape to strip

Things you need:
Big black plastic rubbish bag
6 strips of cardboard, about 2.5 cm wide and 60 cm long
Stiff black paper and sticky tape

22cm   20cm

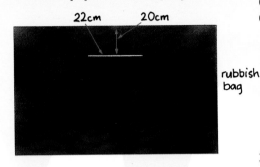

rubbish bag

1 Cut open the black rubbish bag and spread it flat on the floor. Cut a slit for your head, 22 cm long, about 20 cm from the top of the bag, as shown.

2 Lie the six strips of cardboard on top of the bag, like this. Then pull enough of the black plastic over each strip to cover them. Tape the plastic firmly over each strip so they are sealed in.

trim into curves

card tail

3 Trim the edges of the bag in between the strips into curves, using scissors. Cut a tail out of black card and tape it to the middle of the back of the bat shape, as shown.

4 Now put your head through the slit, keeping the tail at the back. Pull the first strip on either side around to the front. Tape them underneath to the wide strip of plastic across your chest.

Batty Ears

Things you need:
Stiff black paper
Hairband and black tape

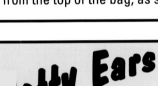

use a grid (see page 5)

1 Cut two ear shapes, like this, out of stiff black paper. Crease them in half along their lengths.

tape on ears

hairband

2 Cover a hairband with black tape. Tape the ears on to the front of the hairband. Pinch up the creases and curve the ears forward.

Hang-About Horrors

Make lots of ghosts to join your party. Drop a small rubber ball, a balloon or even an orange into a pillow case to make the head. Fasten a rubber band loosely around the case under the head. Stick on spooky black eyes. Hang up your horrors with thread or string.

Spooky Tips

Use a spoon to hollow out pumpkins, swedes or turnips. Save the top slices to use as lids. Ask an adult to help you cut out spooky eye, nose and mouth shapes. Put a night-candle inside the pumpkin and make a hole in each lid for the smoke. Light the candles and watch the creepy lantern faces glow in the dark.

Setting the Spooky Scene

To make your party as spooky as possible, eat and play games in a very dark room. Cover the windows with black crêpe paper or black plastic stuck on top of yellow tissue paper. Cut spooky shapes out of the plastic so that the yellow tissue shines through. You can also make a table cover in the same way.

Batty Place Names

Things you need:
Rectangles of stiff black paper,
 each 20 cm by 10 cm
Scissors, pencil and glue
Gold or silver pen

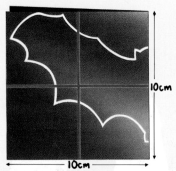

1 Draw this bat shape on a folded rectangle of black paper. Cut it out.

2 Open out the bat and tape a small paperclip on to the end of each wing. Draw around your first bat to make one for every guest. Write on their names.

3 Balance a bat on every cup around the table. Instead of using them as place names, you can also hang or balance your batty bats around the room.

Screamers

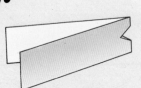

1 Cut a strip of paper, 15 cm long and 3.75 cm wide, for each guest. Fold it in half and snip a triangle out of the fold.

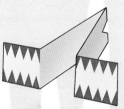

2 Fold back both ends. Open them out against your mouth, gently pressing just behind the triangle with your fingertips. Now blow into the tiny gap between the opened out ends to make a piercing scream.

Ghostie Games

Pass the Coffin

Things you need:
Black card, brown paper and scissors
Sticky tape and a small toy skeleton
Spooky sweets, stickers, red napkin

1 Cut this coffin shape with tabs out of thin black card. Score along the dotted lines. Fold up the tabs and tape them together.

2 Trace around the coffin and cut the shape out. This is the coffin lid. Make a lid for every guest. Tape a lid along one side inside the coffin. Line the coffin with a red napkin and fill it with spooky sweets, stickers and a skeleton. Now you have Drac's coffin.

3 Wrap Drac's coffin in brown paper, taping it underneath. Tape a coffin lid on top and slide a sticker and sweet under it. Wrap all of this in brown paper again, add another lid, sticker and sweet, then wrap again. Carry on until you have wrapped all the lids into the parcel.

How to play:
Everyone sits in a circle in a darkened room. As spooky music plays, they pass the coffin from person to person. The person holding the coffin when the music stops, unwraps the first layer of paper, takes off the lid and eats the sweet. The music starts and stops until everyone has had a turn. The lucky guest who unwraps the real coffin keeps it and the prizes inside it.

To make the game even more fun, write tasks on each lid, such as 'howl three times like a werewolf' or 'walk around the room like a zombie.'

Feely Fun

Everyone sits in a circle in a dark room. The witch has a covered bowl full of things she needs for her spell. They are all parts of a naughty child she caught earlier that day. Really they are things like cauliflower for the child's 'brain', a raw sausage 'finger', peeled grape 'eyes', dried apricot 'ears', spaghetti 'guts' and a slice of ham 'tongue'.

The witch tells her guests that if they are very good, she will let them feel her ingredients in her special feely bag. She then passes round a plastic bag containing one or two spell ingredients at a time, telling everyone in gruesome detail which part of the body they are!

Spooky Bags

For every guest, cut out a black rubbish bag cone shape, 32.5 cm by 42.5 cm, like the one for the witch's hat (see page 13). Curl them into pointed hat shapes and tape the sides. Fold over the top to make a brim. Tape on black paper handles. Fill the bags with batty bats, spooky spiders, sweets, stickers, black balloons and screamers for your ghostie guests to take home.

Grisly grub

To give your spread of grisly grub a ghostly finishing touch, make a table spook for each guest. Use a tangerine as a head and drape an opened-out napkin over it. Fasten a small rubber band around the napkin under the tangerine. Then draw or stick on spooky eyes.

Severed Jelly Hand

Things you need:
Clean rubber glove
2 pegs or bulldog clips
Thin strip of wood
About 280 g lime jelly
Jug of water
Small, sharp scissors

2 Mix the jelly with half the normal amount of water. When it has cooled, pour it into the rubber glove and let it set firmly.

cut open glove

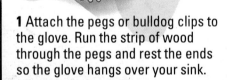

1 Attach the pegs or bulldog clips to the glove. Run the strip of wood through the pegs and rest the ends so the glove hangs over your sink.

3 Put the glove in the freezer away from other food. When it is frozen, carefully cut the glove off using a pair of sharp scissors. To make it look really grisly, drip a few drops of red food colouring on to the wrist of the jelly hand. Keep the hand in the fridge until you are ready to serve it.

Blood and Brains

Serve spaghetti sauce in strong paper cups decorated with skull shapes. Top the sauce with slightly overcooked, chopped spaghetti brains and a dash of tomato sauce blood.

Witch's Brew

Serve limeade or milkshakes made from about 200 ml of ice cold milk per guest whisked together with 2 tablespoons of mint chocolate ice cream. Top them with a scoop of the ice cream and decorate with spooky sweets.

Sliced Spookies

Using scissors, cut out different kinds of spooky shapes from slices of bread. Cover them with cream cheese and add raisin eyes.

Slimy Slugs

Under a medium grill, cook some bananas in their skins for about 10 minutes or until they are brown, turning them once. Make two antennae with cocktail sticks and glacé cherries. Serve them with cream and sugar.

KINGS AND QUEENS PARTY

Your friends will love being royal guests at a kings and queens party where they can dress up in regal robes, cloaks and sashes, crowns and lots of sparkling jewels. Invite them to your party palace decorated with some beautiful banners and flags and ask them to join you in a scrumptious feast of noble nibbles.

INVITATION SCROLLS

KINGS & QUEENS
PARTY
FRIDAY 3rd
4-7pm
JACK
RSVP 0836 2956

1 Write out one invitation on a sheet of white paper, like this. Then ask an adult to photocopy it so that you have a copy for each of your guests.

2 For a special antique look, soak two tea bags in half a cup of warm water. Lay out the invitations on newspaper on a kitchen table or on the floor.

wet teabag

3 Wipe the wet tea bags over each sheet, staining them with the brown tea. Turn the sheets over and stain the other sides. Leave the invitations to dry and then wipe over the edges to make them a darker brown.

roll into scroll

4 Add your guests' names. Roll the invitations up to look like scrolls and tie them with a red ribbon. Then give or post them to your party friends.

You can make your cloaks any size or colour you want.

ROYAL CLOAK

Things you need:
11 (plus spares) coloured bin liners,
  about 75 cm long and 35 cm wide
Bag of cotton wool on a roll
Thin white card and blue tac
Sticky tape, strong glue and scissors

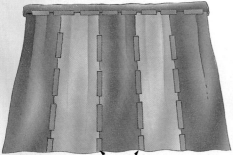

neckband

1 Fold over one bin liner along its length until it is about 5 cm wide. This is the neck band for your cloak.

tape bin liners together

2 Tape the ends of five bin liners along one side of the neck band. Make the bags overlap by about 1 cm. As you tape, gather the ends of the bags slightly making them flare out into a cloak shape. Tape the bags together, overlapping each other, as shown.

tape on second five bin liners

tape bin liners together

3 Turn the cloak over. Tape the next five bin liners on top of the first five, 45 cm from the neck band. Turn the cloak over again and tape the bin liners together side by side, leaving little or no overlap at the bottom so the cloak flares out.

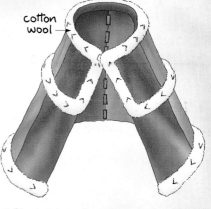

cotton wool

4 Glue strips of cotton wool, about 5 cm wide, around the top part of the cloak. Glue a strip, 10 cm wide, along the bottom of the cloak. Use a black felt tip pen or paper to decorate the wool with V-shapes to make it look like ermine.

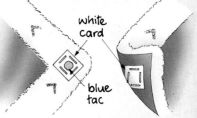

white card

blue tac

5 Staple a 5 cm square of white card on top of one end of the neck band. Staple another square underneath the other end. Stick blue tac to one square. Fasten the cloak by sticking the squares together.

JEWELLED BROOCH

To make a jewelled brooch, cut out a circle of shiny gold paper. Stick on a sweet to look like a jewel.

Fold a long piece of ribbon in half and glue it behind the brooch. Cut a V-shape in the ends of the ribbon. Then fasten the brooch to your cloak or royal sash.

ROYAL WRIST BAND

Make two royal wrist bands from cardboard tubes. Slit the tubes along their lengths. Cut them into 9 cm lengths.

Glue string in a pattern of loops around each tube. Cover the tubes with silver foil and glue on small clear sweets or sequins as jewels.

ROYAL TIP

Mix 3 tablespoons of salt with half a cup of vinegar. Drop lots of copper coins into this mixture.

After a few minutes, the coins will be a lovely, shiny gold colour. Use them as decoration and royal treasure to give to your party guests.

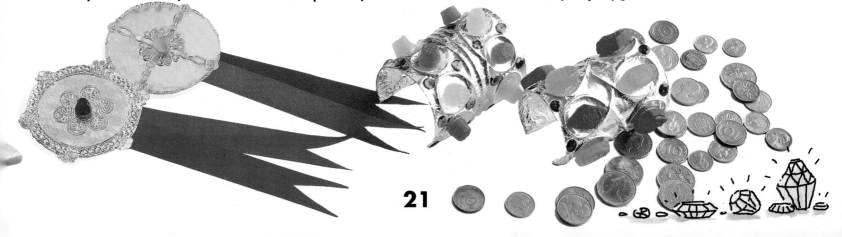

Queen's Skirt

Things you need:
10 or 11 white bin liners,
 75 cm long and 35 cm wide
Red tissue paper
Glue and sticky tape

1 To make a simple wrap-around queen's skirt, follow steps one and two of the royal cloak (see page 21).

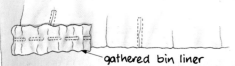

gathered bin liner

2 Make a frill by lying a bin liner along the bottom of the skirt. Gather the bin liner along its middle until it is only about 25 cm long.

tape on frill

3 Tape the gathers in place and then tape the frill to the skirt to make it the right length for you. Add enough frills to go right around the skirt.

tape

4 Glue some red paper tissue bows down the centre of the skirt. Then wrap the skirt around your waist and fasten it at the back with tape.

Fancy Banners

To make a royal banner, fold a long length of rich looking wrapping paper over a wire or coloured coat hanger. Fasten the lower thirds of the paper together. Cut out a big V-shape in the bottom of the banner. Tape the coat hanger to the wall or ceiling. Make banners in different colours and sizes.

Prince's Sash

Fold two long bin liners in half along their lengths. Tape them together to make one long band, about 11 cm wide. Try the band on for size and then tape or staple it together where it crosses over.

Cut both ends to make them pointed. Fold under and tape the points to make them look neat. Then glue a jewelled brooch (see page 21) on to the sash.

Royal Crown

Things you need:
Thin gold card or plain card
 covered with gold paper
Red crêpe paper, 45 cm by 50 cm
8 cm square of paper
Roll of cotton wool
Clear sweets for jewels
Black felt tip pen
Scissors, glue and sticky tape

6cm

1 To make the headband, cut a strip of card, 6 cm wide, to fit around your head. Tape the ends together.

 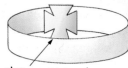

cut out corner

glue on cross shape

2 Fold the paper square in half and in half again. Snip out the corner opposite the fold. Unfold the paper into a cross shape. Draw around it on to gold card. Then cut it out and glue it in place on the headband.

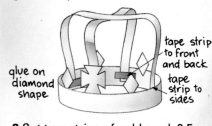

glue on diamond shape

tape strip to front and back

tape strip to sides

3 Cut two strips of gold card, 2.5 cm wide and 50 cm long. Tape them to the headband, as shown. Cut four 3.5 cm diamond shapes out of gold card and glue them round the band.

clear sweet

cotton wool strip

4 Push the crêpe paper up into the crown. Tape it in place. Glue cotton wool round the outside of the band. Decorate it with V-shapes. Glue on sweets and sequins as jewels.

Castle Capers

Why not play some crazy castle games with your party friends. Here are three really easy games which need hardly any preparation but are great fun to play. To make you feel like real kings and queens, play them in a room hung with lots of brightly coloured royal banners and sit on regal looking cushions.

Pass The Ring

Sit all your guests in a circle with one person in the middle. Thread a ring on to a piece of string long enough for them all to hold. Then tie the ends together.

Everyone grips the string with both hands. The person in the middle must not look while somebody secretly covers the ring with one hand.

The game is for everyone to pass the ring around the circle, or pretend to pass it even if they don't have it under their hand. The person in the middle tries to guess who has the ring. When she guesses correctly, the person with the ring changes places and sits in the middle and the game goes on.

Queenie, Queenie

One person is Queenie and stands at one end of the room with her back facing the other players. Everyone else lines up at the other end of the room. They shout, 'Queenie, Queenie, can we come to your castle?' Queenie replies, 'Yes, but only if you're wearing .....' and says a colour, say blue, purple, red or black. Anyone wearing the colour takes one step forward.

The game continues with Queenie calling out different colours until someone is close enough to touch her. Everyone dashes back to get in line while Queenie tries to catch one of them. Whoever she catches becomes the next Queenie.

Royal Thimbles

For this royal game, you will need two thimbles and one drinking straw for each of your guests.

To play the game, divide your guests into teams of equal numbers. The last person in each team pretends to be the Queen. The other guests are not allowed to touch their Queen's royal thimble. Instead, each one holds a straw in his teeth. On the word 'go', a thimble must be passed down each team from straw to straw until it reaches the Queen. If a thimble is dropped, it must go back to the beginning again.

The first team to place its thimble on their Queen's little finger is the winner.

NOBLE NIBBLES

Serve a mini banquet on a plush red table cover with gold and silver paper place mats and shining knives, spoons and forks. Make golden napkin rings from thin sections of cardboard rolls covered with gold paper and sequins. Toast your guests with rich red fruit juice.

CASTLE CAKE

Buy six rectangular-shaped cakes, already covered in icing or marzipan. (Battenburg cakes are best). Cut two in half and position them with the other cakes to make a castle shape, as shown in the photograph.

Make 115 g of butter icing (it is made the same way as for the treasure islands on page 11) and add pink food colouring. Cover four ice cream cones with most of the icing and sprinkle them carefully with lots of hundreds and thousands. Spread a little icing on the top of each tower. Use more icing to stick jelly diamond cake decorations around the towers.

Stick on chocolate wafer mints in the same way to make a castle drawbridge. Stand an ice cream cone on top of each tower.

CASTLE FLAGS

Cut pennant shapes and small triangles from red ribbon or paper. Thread the triangles on to cotton and string them between the towers. Fasten the red pennants to cocktail sticks and push one into the top of each tower.

MELON CROWNS

Ask an adult to help you cut yellow melons into crown-shaped halves. Slice off the bottoms so they stand upright. Scoop out the seeds and then fill the centres with cherries, grapes or strawberries to look like jewels. Put the crowns on the table ready to cut into servings for your friends.

CASTLE LAWNS

Spread a thin layer of butter icing around the base of your cake. Pour about 25 g of desiccated coconut into a small plastic bag. Add a few drops of bright green food colouring and shake the bag until the coconut has turned green. Scatter the coconut so it completely covers the butter icing.

JEWELLED GOBLETS

Things you need:
Paper cups
Larger, clear plastic cups
(The bases of the plastic and paper cups should be about the same size)
Kitchen foil
Small clear sweets for jewels
Craft knife and sticky tape

2 Turn the paper cups upside down. Ask an adult to help cut slits around each cup, like this.

squeeze in and tape

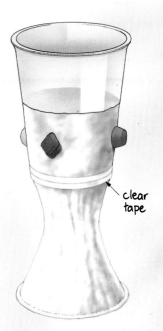

clear tape

1 Use a plastic and paper cup for each guest. Wrap all but the top part of each plastic cup in kitchen foil. Tape it in place underneath the cup and where it overlaps at the side.

3 Squeeze each paper cup in the middle and tape it in place so that it looks like an egg cup. These are the goblet stems. Wrap each stem in kitchen foil and tape it in place underneath the base.

4 Tape the paper and plastic cups neatly together, base to base. Glue lots of small clear sweets around the goblets to look like sparkling jewels.

JEWELLED DAINTIES

Spread round, plain biscuits with butter or cream cheese. Top them with raisins, glacé cherries and cake decorations to look like sparkling jewels.

SAVOURY SHIELDS

Use scissors to cut slices of bread into shield shapes. Cover them with cheese slices trimmed to fit or with cream cheese. Cut strips or slices of ham, cheese, sausages, celery, cucumber and carrots to create smart shield designs.

ROYALLED EGGS

Gently boil some eggs for about ten minutes. When they are cool, draw royal designs on their shells with brightly coloured felt tip pens. Stand each egg in a cardboard napkin band covered with gold paper and decorated with sequins.

ALIEN PARTY

An alien party will give your friends a chance to dress up in really crazy, out-of-this-world outfits.

Send them each a rocket invitation and ask them to come as galactic gleepers, zargon fighters, Venus vegoids or other weird visitors from outer space. At the end of the party, give a funny prize to the strangest alien of all.

ROCKET INVITE

1 Cut a triangle with sides about 18 cm long from thin coloured card, or use card covered with foil or painted silver. Do one for each of your guests. Fold the triangles in half, as shown.

thin card

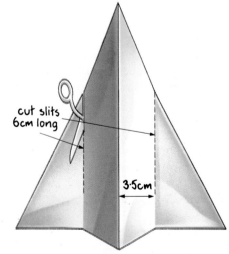

cut slits 6cm long

3·5cm

2 Turn back the bottom corners, making a crease 3.5 cm from the fold. Cut a 6 cm slit down each crease. Half open up each triangle and stand them up, as shown.

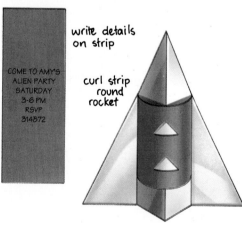

write details on strip

curl strip round rocket

COME TO AMY'S ALIEN PARTY SATURDAY 3-6 PM RSVP 314872

3 Write out the party details on a strip of paper, 6 cm wide and 16 cm long. Make a copy for every guest. Curl the strip around the rocket, inside the slits, like this, and tape the ends. Add each guest's name on the outside.

GALACTIC BODY ARMOUR

Things you need:
Thin coloured card and stiff paper
Scissors, ruler and sticky tape

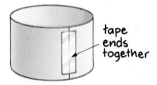

tape ends together

1 Cut two strips of card, 7 cm wide and long enough to fit around the tops of your arms. Make sure they are loose enough to fit over a tight fitting top. Tape the ends to make two armbands.

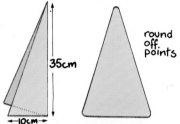

35cm

10cm

round off points

2 Cut two big triangles, 20 cm wide and 35 cm high. Round off the points.

tape

3 To make shoulder spikes, tape a triangle to the inside of each armband, as shown. Wear the armbands so the triangles stick up above your shoulders.

shoulder spike

elbow spike

knee spike

4 Cut four triangles 15 cm wide and 25 cm high. Use two to make elbow spikes. These spikes should stick out backwards from bands below your elbows. Use the other two to make knee spikes to stick up over your knees from bands around your calves.

GALACTIC GLEEPER

Things you need:
A pair of coloured nylon tights
2 balloons, cotton wool and thin card
2 ping pong balls or big, round plastic bottle tops

Blow up the two balloons until they are each about the size of a tennis ball. Push one balloon into the top of each leg of the coloured tights. Pull the tights over your head and ears. Then push the balloons slightly apart.

Put the ping pong balls on your forehead and pull the waistband of the tights over them to hold them in place. To make it more comfortable, place a wad of cotton wool under each ball. Wrap the legs of the tights around the bottom of each balloon, neatly tucking under the ends. Then tuck in all your hair. Add card eyes.

STAR TIPS

To complete your alien outfits, wear close-fitting tops, and tights or track suit bottoms, tucked into plain boots. To make them look spacy, wear knee spikes around the tops of the boots.

For a real alien look, wrap cling film over your clothes. Wrap it around your waist, over your shoulders and down your legs and arms. Tape it in place.

GALACTIC GRABBERS

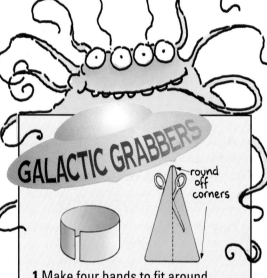

round off corners

1 Make four bands to fit around your wrists and ankles. Cut out four triangles, 15 cm wide and 25 cm high. Round off their corners and cut the triangles in half.

tape

2 Tape two halves of a triangle to each band, with their ends overlapping, as shown.

ankle grabber

wrist grabber

3 Fasten the bands around your wrists and ankles with paper clips or tape. Fold up the ankle grabbers slightly to go over your feet. Wear the wrist bands so the grabbers go over the back of your hands.

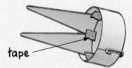

VENUS VEGOID

Things you need:
Green and blue crêpe paper
Thin card and stiff paper
Felt-tipped pens
Scissors, ruler and sticky tape

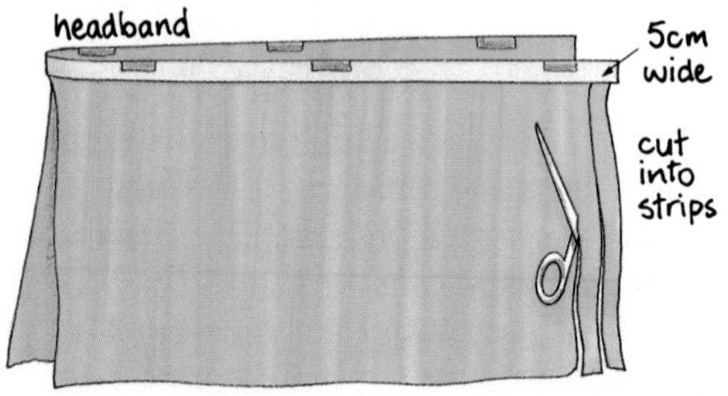

headband
5cm wide
cut into strips

1 Cut a strip of card 5 cm wide and long enough to go around your head. Tape two layers of blue crêpe paper, about 50 cm wide, along the band. Cut the paper into strips 2 cm wide.

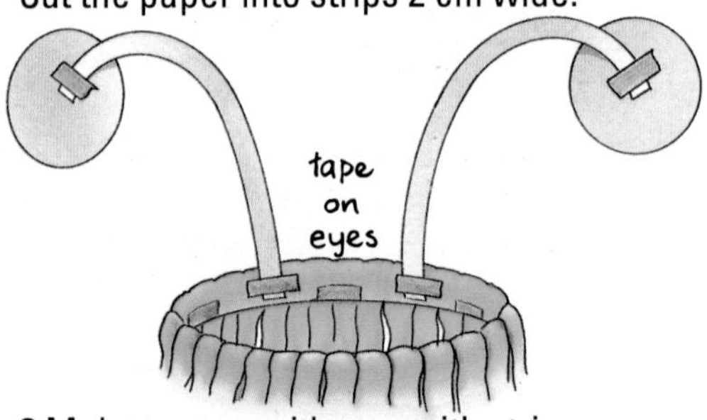

tape on eyes

2 Make two vegoid eyes with strips of card 25 cm long and 1.5 cm wide. Colour circles of stiff paper, 7.5 cm across, to look like eyes. Tape them to one end of each strip. Tape the other ends of the strips to the inside of the front of the headband.

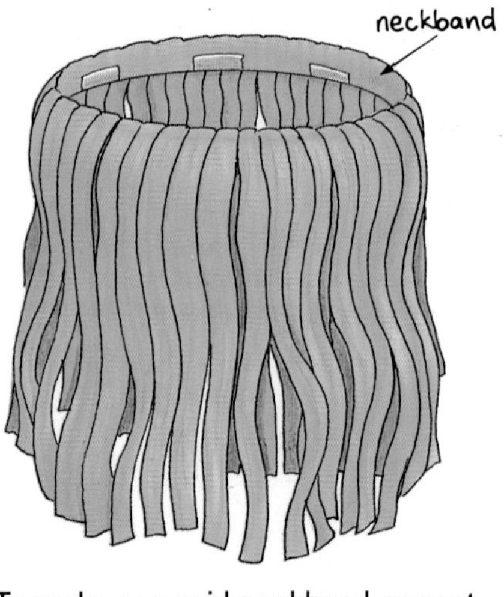

neckband

3 To make a vegoid neckband, repeat steps one and two but make the band big enough to go over your head and rest on your shoulders. Use green crêpe paper this time.

wrist band

knee band

4 Make vegoid knee bands in the same way, using green crêpe paper, about 30 cm wide. Make wrist and ankle bands using blue crêpe paper. Fasten the bands with paper clips.

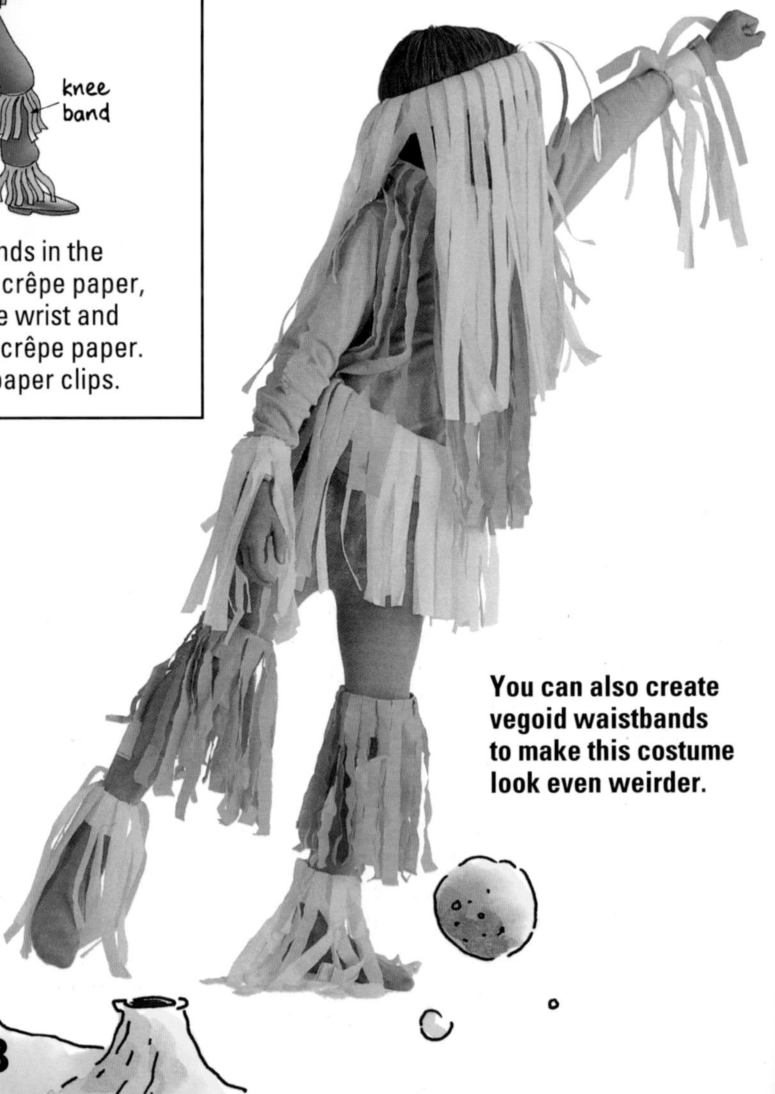

SPACE TIP

Make antennae with two long, thin triangles of card, each 2.5 cm wide at the base, tapering to 32 cm long. Make them wavy by dragging them between your first finger and thumb. Tape them inside the front of your headband.

You can also create vegoid waistbands to make this costume look even weirder.

ZARGON FIGHTER TOP

Things you need:
A strong rubbish bag
Scissors, silver foil and glue
Ruler and pencil

mark out triangle

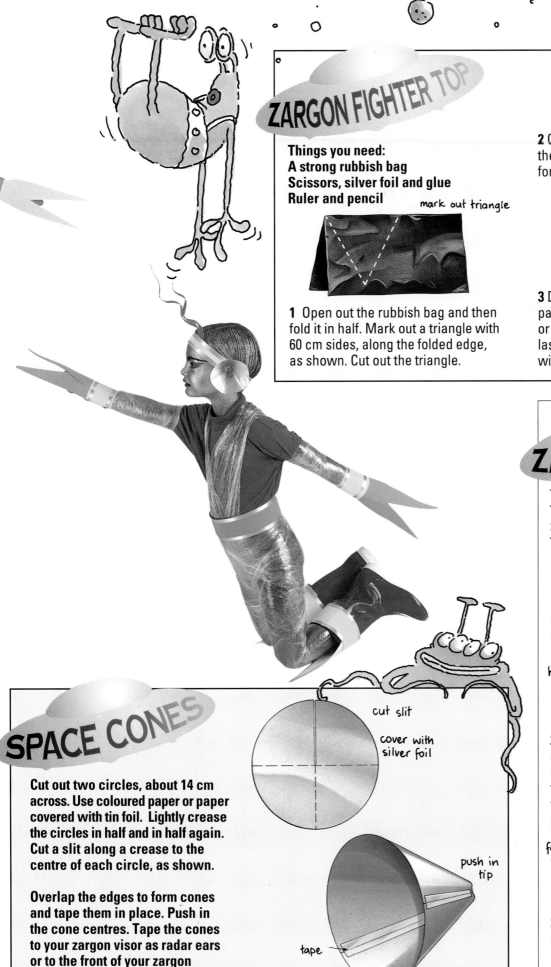

1 Open out the rubbish bag and then fold it in half. Mark out a triangle with 60 cm sides, along the folded edge, as shown. Cut out the triangle.

cut slit

2 Cut a slit, about 20 cm long, along the centre of the fold to make a hole for your head to go through.

decorate with silver foil

3 Decorate your fighter's top with patterns made from strips of silver foil or gold paper and add a space cone laser. Wear it over a high-necked top with a colourful zargon visor.

ZARGON VISOR

Things you need:
Thin card or stiff paper
Scissors, ruler and sticky tape
Two paper fasteners

tape   ear marks   ↕ 3cm

1 Cut a band of card 3 cm wide to fit over your ears and around your forehead. Tape the ends together and mark the position of your ears.

headband   visor   eye slits

2 Measure the length from ear to ear along the front of the headband. Cut another 3 cm wide strip of card this length to make a visor. Put the visor over your eyes and mark their position. Then cut two thin eye slits.

fasten visor to band   headband

3 Fasten the ends of the visor to the headband just in front of your ears, using paper fasteners. Now you can move it up and down.

SPACE CONES

Cut out two circles, about 14 cm across. Use coloured paper or paper covered with tin foil. Lightly crease the circles in half and in half again. Cut a slit along a crease to the centre of each circle, as shown.

Overlap the edges to form cones and tape them in place. Push in the cone centres. Tape the cones to your zargon visor as radar ears or to the front of your zargon fighter top as lasers.

cut slit

cover with silver foil

push in tip

tape

ORBITING OBJECTS

To make your alien party house look more like outer-space, string up some sparkling star trails. Cut out lots of paper or card stars and give them a glue and glitter sparkle. Then string them together on lengths of thread. Make each star trail lead to a room labelled with the name of a faraway planet.

SKY SCANNER

Things you need:
2 medium tinfoil pie tins
2 space cones (see page 29)
2 drinking straws
Stapler and thread

space cone — pie tin

1 Tape a space cone to the bottom of each pie tin, as shown.

straw antennae

2 To make the antennae, fold the straws in half. Poke the ends through holes in the middle of the cones and then through the pie tins. Snip off the ends of the straws inside the tins.

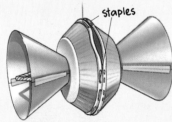

staples

3 Staple the pie tins together around their rims, leaving a large opening. Hang up each scanner by a long piece of thread from a staple at one end of the opening.

Make enough scanners for every guest. Label them and fill them with small spacy treats to take home.

SKY ROCKETS

Using thin card covered with silver foil, follow the steps for the rocket invites (see page 26). Use coloured paper to curl round the rocket. Hang the rockets up by a long thread in the tail end and a shorter one in the tip.

Tape a long strip of cling film to the tail end. Stretch it out and tape the end to the wall, making the cling film look like the rocket's smoky trail.

ROBO CUPS

You'll need two paper cups for each of your alien guests. Poke two holes in the bottom of one cup and push a straw through each hole.

Stand this cup upside down on top of the other one. Tape it in place so the top cup is hinged to the bottom one. Then add two eyes, grids and controls. Tip back the top cup to fill the bottom one with a spacy drink.

GALAXY GAMES

FORCEFIELD RESCUE

Ask an adult to knot two or three old sheets together very firmly. Ask for two or three volunteer spacemen, all about the same size. Get them to stand about two steps apart from each other.

Ask the adult to tie the sheets very firmly in a loop around the middles of the spacemen. This is the forcefield.

Place a teddy bear or doll a step or two away from each spaceman, just outside the forcefield.

When you say 'go', the spacemen must all stretch out and push against the forcefield to try and grab their teddy or doll. The first one to grab on to and rescue his own teddy or doll is the winning spaceman and gets a prize.

SATELLITE SPINNERS

Things you need:
Stiff paper and scissors
Felt tip pens and a ruler

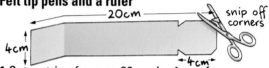

20cm

4cm

snip off corners

4cm

1 Cut a strip of paper, 20 cm by 4 cm, for every guest. Fold over the last 4 cm of the ends of each strip. Snip off all the corners, as shown.

ANNA

draw on lines

2 Rule lines down and across both sides of the folded ends to make them look like satellite solar panels. Glue different coloured triangles in the centre of both sides . Write a guest's name on each satellite.

ANNA

3 Use the satellites as place names, then let your guests toss them gently in the air. Watch the satellites spin and their triangles flicker.

SPACE RACE

Make two space cones from circles 12 cm across and decorate them like lunar modules. Thread each one on to about two metres of thread or string. Tie one end of each string to the back of a chair and the other ends to the back of another chair. Move the chairs apart, pulling the strings tight.

Push each lunar module about 25 cm down its string.

Two teams of guests can then race them, taking it in turns to blow them through space to the end of each string.

IN FLIGHT FOOD

To give your alien party just the right atmosphere, create a space scene to hang up or to use as a table cover. Use glue to paint swirly galaxy shapes and planet rings on a big black cloth or rubbish bag, opened out flat. Sprinkle silver and gold glitter over the glue. When it is dry, carefully shake off the spare glitter. Then cut out and stick on lots of different sized paper circles to look like planets.

KRISPIE CRATERS

Things you need:
750 g milk chocolate
300-350 g Rice Krispies
1 large cake base
A glass
Green jelly babies

melt chocolate

1 You might need to ask an adult to help you. Melt about 200 g of chocolate at a time. Break it into pieces and stir it in a bowl standing in a large pan of hot water over a low heat.

pour in melted chocolate

2 Pour the melted chocolate into a mixing bowl and add some of the Rice Krispies. Keep adding and stirring Rice Krispies into the chocolate until the mixture is quite stiff.

3 Repeat steps one and two until all the chocolate is melted and cannot absorb any more of the Rice Krispies. You will have to work quite fast to keep the mixture warm.

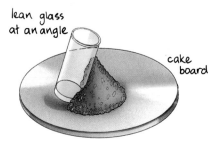
lean glass at an angle
cake board

4 This step is sticky and messy but fun. Spoon out some of the mixture on to the cake board and mould it into a mound. Grease the glass and lean it at an angle against the mound.

krispie craters
jelly babies

5 Build up the mixture around the glass into a volcano shape. Use the rest to make craters, as shown. Remove the glass as the craters begin to set. Add a flag and little green jelly baby aliens.

CRASHED ROCKET CAKE

Use a small Swiss roll about the same diameter as the glass used in the Krispie Craters. Stiffen it with a skewer pushed lengthways through the centre. Cover it with ready-made icing, or about 85 g of plain butter icing (see page 11). Add a little blue food colouring to the icing left over from this recipe.

Cut four wafers diagonally to make rocket fins. Cover them with the blue icing. Then push them into slits cut around one end of the Swiss roll rocket.

Lean the rocket inside the volcano shaped Krispie Crater. Add bootlace liquorice as damaged rocket wiring and rocket stripes. Stick on a number and some candles, as shown.

SPACE SPUDS

Serve baked potatoes wrapped in foil. Push in three cocktail sticks as legs. Push the end of each leg into a slice of carrot to act as a base. Serve the potatoes with butter, cheese, salad or prawns.

FLYING SAUCER SERVERS

Use two medium-sized paper bowls for every flying saucer. Poke two holes in the bottom of one bowl. Push a straw down one hole and up through the other so the ends of the straw stick out from the base of the bowl.

Put the bowl upside-down on top of the other one. Then hinge the bowls by stapling the top one in place. Stick on or draw lots of spaceship details. Then fill the bottom bowl with in-flight food.

COSMIC DOUGHNUTS

Push a marshmallow into the centre of a ring doughnut. Spike a marshmallow on to one end of four cocktail sticks and push in the sticks around the edge of the doughnut. Tie thread to each stick and hang the doughnut above the party table. Make a few to serve whole or cut them into quarters for your guests to eat.

STARWICHES

Use a star-shaped pastry cutter to punch out star-shaped sandwiches. Fill the sandwiches before you cut them out. Put starwiches in flying saucer servers to give to your alien guests.

POP STAR PARTY

Ask your friends to dress up as their favourite pop star in really cool or glamorous gear jazzed up with lots of funky jewellery. Set the scene by making your house look like a fun disco with all kinds of coloured lights, glittering decorations, shiny balloons and loud pop star music.

HIP HAT INVITE

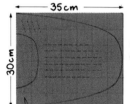

35 cm

30 cm

draw on dotted lines

1 Draw this hip hat shape and the dotted lines on a sheet of coloured paper, about 30 cm wide and 35 cm long.

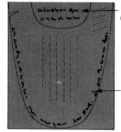

write "cut along dotted line".... here

write on party details

2 Write the party details along the sides of the hat shape. At the top, write,'CUT ALONG THE DOTTED LINES. CURL THE ENDS AROUND AND FIT THE NOTCH INTO ONE OF THE SLITS TO FIT YOUR HEAD.' Make one hat for each guest.

decorate hat

roll up invitation

guest's name

3 Add one of the guest's name to the front of each hat. Decorate the hats with glitter, sequins and stars and then roll them up and send them out as invitations. Ask each guest to wear a hat to your party.

DISCO DRESS

Things you need:
2 large plastic rubbish bags
Sticky tape and scissors
Chalk or a pencil

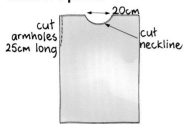

1 Lay one rubbish bag out flat. Cut a neckline 20 cm across, as shown, in the end of the bag. For the armholes, cut a slit in each side, 25 cm long.

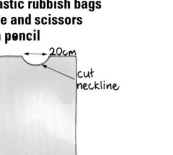

2 Put the hole in the bag over your head. Then tuck up and tape the ends of the bag between your legs. Fold under and tape up the ends of the bag around each leg to make balloon pants.

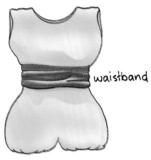

3 Cut a waistband, about 150 cm long and 44 cm wide, from the second bag. Fold it in half lengthways. Then tie it around your waist, like a belt.

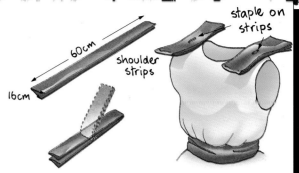

4 Make shoulder straps from two strips of plastic, 60 cm long and 16 cm wide. Fold them in half lengthways. Fold them in half again and again so they are about 15 cm long. Staple one to each shoulder.

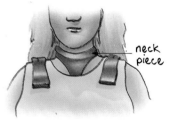

5 Cut a 35 cm triangle from the second bag. Tuck one point into the top of your dress, as shown. Tape the other two points together at the back of your neck. Add wrist bands made from plastic strips 24 cm wide, folded in half.

FUNKY RAPPER

To look like a rapper, wear a hooded sweat shirt and old jeans decorated with paper shapes stuck on with fabric glue. Add chunky trainers, dark glasses and a headband or baseball cap turned the wrong way round. Wear a gold chain and lots of bright badges.

PUNK ROCKER

Cut triangles round the armholes and neck of an old black T-shirt. Add lots of home-made gold studs and wear strands of brilliant beads (see page 36) around your neck. Wrap a chunky belt around your waist.

Girls can decorate a short skirt with studs and badges and wear it with coloured tights. Boys can cut slashes over the thigh and knee of a pair of old tight-fitting jeans. They can cover them with studs and wear old canvas shoes.

DANCE MIKE

Colour a bendy straw with a black permanent marker. Crumple a 14 cm square of silver foil into a ball and roll it up tight between the palms of your hands. Poke a small hole in the ball and push it on to the end of the straw.

Tape the straw to the headband of a pair of personal stereo earphones so the ball is in front of your mouth. Now you are ready to sing while you dance.

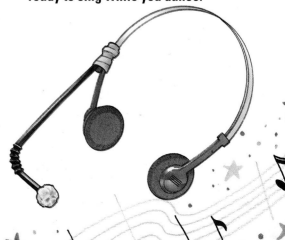

FUNKY JEWELLERY

Create lots of funky chains from silver or coloured paperclips, drinking straws or triangles of colourful wrapping paper. Join them together or thread them on to strong cotton or thin elastic and wear them round your neck, wrists and ankles. Turn them into earrings by tying on loops of thread to go around your ears.

You can make shiny stud patterns on your costumes with paper fasteners, but cover the ends with tape to stop them from scratching. Brighten up the buttons on your clothes, too, by covering them with paper cut-outs of your favourite pop stars or film stars.

Jazz up your necklaces with more beads made from 5 cm squares of silver foil crumpled into balls, or colourful drinking straws cut into short lengths.

BRILLIANT BEADS

wrapping paper

5cm

30cm long

1 Cut long triangles, about 5 cm wide and tapering to 30 cm long, from old magazine pages or colourful wrapping paper, like this.

wrap around straw

2 Starting from the wide end of each triangle, roll them around a very thin drinking straw, as shown, or with your fingers until you reach the tip.

glue down end

3 Dab a little glue on to the end of each triangle and stick it down. You need about twelve beads for a necklace.

thread beads together

4 Thread the beads through the holes on to some thin elastic or wool. Or make a hole through one tip to pull the wool through so the beads hang downwards.

HOT TIPS

Work hair mousse or gel into your hair to create a spiky style. Then use a damp sponge or an old toothbrush to paint in jazzy streaks of water-based face paints.

Look out for second-hand clothes, such as big jackets, waistcoats and shirts. Use badges, keys and belts as well as funky jewellery to turn them into stylish pop star outfits.

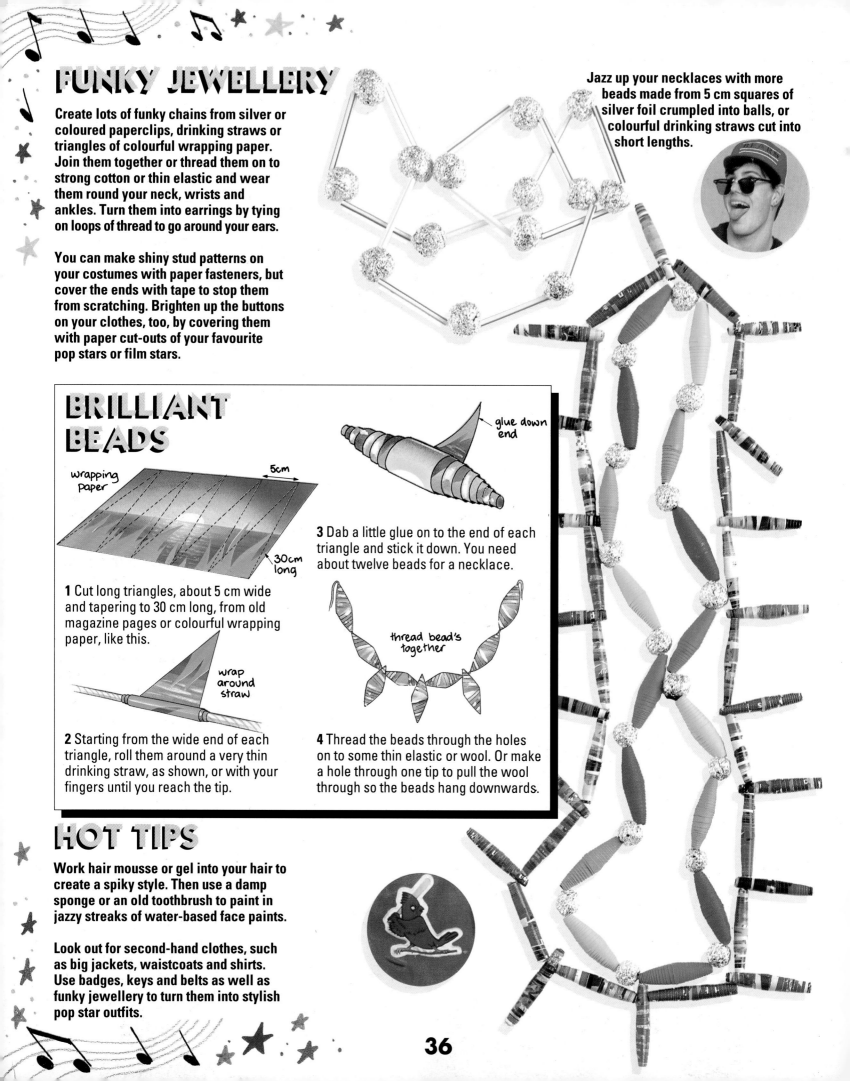

FAB FUN

Turn your party room into a dance floor and burn off lots of energy with your friends as you play these pop star party games to the latest hit songs.

BALLOON STOMP

Tie a balloon to one of each of your guest's ankles. Play your favourite pop song and tell everyone to get stomping in time to the music. The winner is the last guest with an unpopped balloon.

STAR TURN

To play this game, guests take it in turn to pretend to be a pop star. Everyone else has to guess who they are by asking them to do something in the style of the star. These tasks can be things like washing dishes, brushing their hair, directing traffic or cleaning their teeth.

DRESS-UP DASH

This game is really musical chairs played with clothes. Place a line of things to wear in the centre of the room. These can be clothes and sunglasses, shoes or belts. There must be one less item of clothing than there are guests.

Put on some music and get your guests to dance around the clothes. When the music stops they must all try to grab something from the pile and put it on. The one who is left without anything to put on is out.

Lay out another line of clothes, again with one item less than the number of players. Start the music again. Everyone starts dancing, wearing the clothes they picked up.

The whole game is repeated with one less item of clothing each time until there is only one guest left. Of course, she is wearing lots of different crazy looking clothes.

FAR OUT FOOD

To give your pop star party food a musical touch, create a keyboard cover for the table. Use a black felt tip pen or thin black tape to make the black keys. Draw or stick them on to longs strips of white paper. Cover your table with a table cloth and tape the strips on top, around the edges.

MARSHMALLOW MIKES

To make a marshmallow mike, thread a length of bootlace liquorice through the end of an ice cream cone, knotting the end inside.

Carefully push a coconut-topped marshmallow into the top of the cone. You may need to slice off the bottom of the marshmallow.

ROCKING ROOSTERS

Cover the top and bottom rims of a biscuit tin with bands of silver foil. Then wrap a brightly coloured strip of crêpe paper around the tin and tape it in place.

Decorate the crêpe with strips of folded silver foil as shown in the photograph. Then cover the top of the tin with a circle of greaseproof paper.

Serve chicken drumsticks coated with a breadcrumb mixture on the upturned tin. Wrap red paper cut into thin strips and a strip of silver foil around each drumstick to make them look really smart.

You could also cook different kinds of coloured pasta shapes, tossed in oil to make them glisten. Serve up a delicious fresh tomato sauce to go with them.

FAB FLOATS

Top glasses of coloured fizzy drinks like orange, cherry and lime, with scoops of tutti frutti or vanilla ice cream. Add straws and cocktail decorations to each ice cream float.

JAZZY JELLIES

Stand a drinking glass in a plastic food tub. Carefully tip the glass so one side rests on the edge of the tub. Mix the jelly, let it cool a little and then pour it carefully into the glass. When the jelly has set, tip the glass on its other side and pour in another coloured jelly.

When the jelly is completely set, top it with whipped cream, hundreds and thousands and glacé cherries. Make lots of jellies at the same time and use custard mixes too, for even more colour.

FLASH IN THE PAN

Things you need:
150 g digestive biscuit crumbs
25 g butter
25 g golden syrup
75 g desiccated coconut
3 strawberries and 2 bananas
1 orange segment
Lemon juice

add crumbs

1 Melt the butter in a pan over a low heat. Add the syrup and the crumbs. Stir gently over a low heat until the crumbs are coated with butter.

pour on coconut

2 Pour the mixture into a pie dish and flatten it to cover the bottom of the dish. Pour the coconut over the top and flatten it as well.

design flash pattern

3 Use a knife to draw a flash pattern, like this, in the coconut. Slice enough strawberries into thin lengths to go around the edge of the pattern.

banana slices *strawberry slices* *orange segment*

4 Thinly slice the bananas and the rest of the strawberries. Arrange the strawberry slices inside the pattern and the banana ones outside. Put the orange segment in place, as shown. Serve the pie chilled, with lashings of cream or scoops of vanilla ice cream.

POPCORN PAGES

Roll magazine pages into cones. Tape them in place. Fill each one with popcorn and serve them to your pop star guests.

Jungle Party

Give a jungle party and ask your guests to come as wild animals, like these crazy crocodiles, lazy lions, leopards and zany zebras. For a true jungle feel, hang real or crêpe paper leaves, paper vines and slithery snakes around the house. Have a tape of bird or animal noises playing in the background.

Snakey Invite

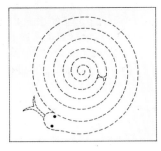

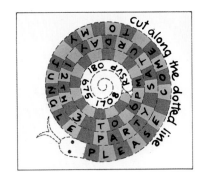

hang up snake

1 Draw a spiral snake shape with a dotted line, like this, on a piece of paper small enough to fit into an envelope. Add a forked tongue. Draw one snake for each guest.

2 Write each guest's name and your party details inside the curves. Make the end a reply slip. Write 'cut along the dotted line' beside the snake's head. Decorate each invitation.

3 Put the invitations into envelopes and send them to your friends. When they cut along the dotted lines, their invitations will turn into paper snakes which they can hang up.

Crazy Croc Cap

Things you need:
Thin card and green crêpe paper
Yellow and black felt tip pens
Scissors, sticky tape and glue stick

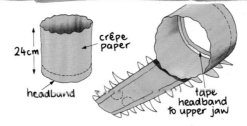

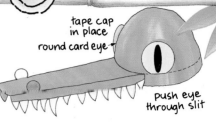

cut out nostril flaps

10cm

35cm

1 To make the upper jaw, cut out this shape from a sheet of white or yellow card folded in half. Use a grid (see page 5). Cut around the nostril flaps. Draw around the upper jaw to make the lower jaw shape. Cut it out.

cover jaws in green crêpe paper

cut 1.5cm slits

2 Cover the jaws in crêpe paper. Leave the teeth white or yellow.

24cm — crêpe paper

headband

tape headband to upper jaw

3 Make a headband to fit your head from a strip of card 3 cm wide. Tape a strip of crêpe paper, about 24 cm wide, to the headband. Tape the ends together. Then tape the headband to the upper jaw.

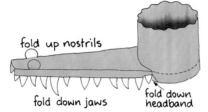

fold up nostrils

fold down jaws

fold down headband

4 Cut slits 1.5 cm long from the edge of the jaw on both sides, as shown. Fold down along the dotted lines. Fold the headband down and the nostrils up.

tape cap in place
round card eye

push eye through slit

5 To make the cap, fold the crêpe paper over your head. Tape it in place on the inside. Cut a slit in each side of the cap. Push a yellow eye into each slit, as shown, and tape them inside.

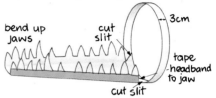

bend up jaws

cut slit

3cm

tape headband to jaw

cut slit

6 Make a headband to go under your chin from thin card 3 cm wide. Tape it under the end of the lower jaw. Cut 1.5 cm slits from the edges, under the band. Fold the teeth up along the sides, as shown.

Crazy Croc Tail

Things you need:
Sheets of paper
Green crêpe paper
Sticky tape, scissors, craft knife, stapler and glue stick

1 Cut out a sheet of paper, 30 cm by 40 cm. This is the top half of the tail.

15cm

115cm

2 Tape together enough sheets of paper to make a big sheet 30 cm wide and 115 cm long. This is the bottom half of the tail. Fold it in half and cut out the shape, as shown.

30cm

40cm

tape top and bottom together

cut out v-shapes

3 Cover both sections in green crêpe paper. Then cut out little V-shapes along their lengths, as shown, to look like spikes. Tape the sections together.

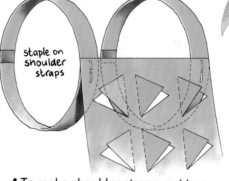

staple on shoulder straps

4 To make shoulder straps, cut two strips of crêpe paper 60 cm x 20 cm. Fold them in half along their lengths and in half again so they are 5 cm wide. Staple one strip to each side of the top of the croc's tail. Tape the ends of each strip together to make a loop that will fit over your shoulders.

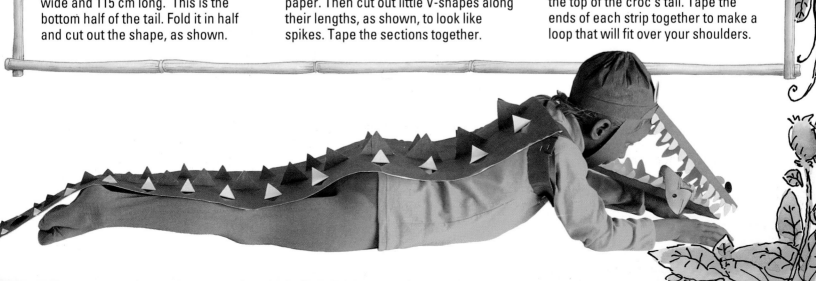

Lazy Lion Mane

Things you need:
2 strips of thin card, 3 cm wide and long enough to go over your head
2 pieces of yellow crêpe paper, 75 cm wide and as long as the strips of card
2 pieces of yellow crêpe paper, 25 cm wide and as long as the strips of card
1 m yellow ribbon
Scissors and stapler

staple on ribbon

cut into strips

2 Cut two strips of ribbon, each 25 cm long. Staple one to each end of the card strip. Cut the crêpe into strips 2 cm wide, to make a mane.

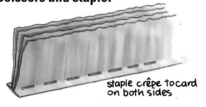

staple crêpe to card on both sides

1 Lay the two 75 cm sheets of crêpe on top of each other. Lay the card strip along the middle of the crêpe paper. Fold the crêpe over the strip and staple it in place, as shown.

tie ribbon under chin

3 Make the second part of the mane in the same way, using the 25 cm crêpe paper sheets. Wearing your mask, wrap the short mane round your head, then the long one. Tie them under your chin.

Jungle Tips

The best way to keep your tail on is to staple the middle of a length of ribbon, about 75 cm long, on to the end without the tuft. Tie the ribbon around your waist with the tail at the back.

Wear a green top and tights for the crazy croc, yellow for the leopard and yellow or brown for the lazy lion. Cut out big and small spots from sticky-backed black plastic to cover the leopard's back, legs and tail. Stick orange paper spots in the centre of each big spot.

Zebras need black and white stripy tops and white tights. Use black tape to make leg stripes and black shoes and gloves for hooves.

Jungle Masks

Zebra

Lion

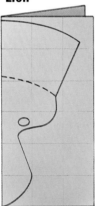

Leopard

Zebra ear

The squares on these grids are all 5 cm x 5 cm.

Lion ear

To form the ears, pinch the ends together. Tape down the flap you make underneath.

Leopard ear

Fasten the ears to their masks with sticky tape or glue.

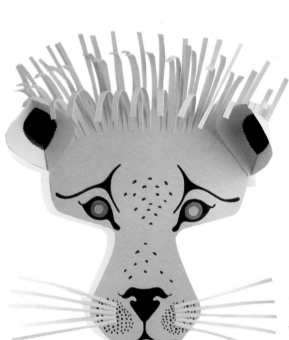

Cut out the masks and ears from thin card folded in half, using the patterns above. To make them the exact size, it is best to draw them on a grid (see page 5).

Open out the masks, draw on the eyes, noses and other features. Glue on the lion and leopard ears and long thin strips of white card for whiskers. Cut out small eye holes. Cut the lion mask fringe. Then tape headbands behind the lion and leopard masks.

For the zebra, make a headband cap like the crocodile's (see page 41) with white crêpe paper. Tape it behind the mask. Tape the zebra ears to the headband.

Zany Zebra Mane

Things you need:
Stiff black paper and white paper
Sticky tape, stapler, scissors

10cm
21cm
tape

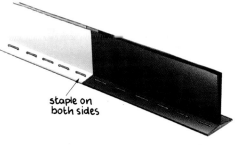

cut into strips
tape mane to cap
add black strips

1 Cut five pieces of black paper and four of white paper, each measuring 10 cm x 21 cm. Tape the pieces of paper together along their lengths to make one long black and white strip.

staple on both sides

2 Stick a long piece of tape along the centre of the black and white strip. Fold the edges of the paper round the tape and staple them to the tape, as shown.

3 Cut the strip into a gentle curve and then cut it into thin strips to make a fringe. Tape the mane to the top of the zebra cap. Add black stripes to the cap.

Zebra Tail

Things you need:
Thin white card
Stiff black paper
Black sticky tape
Sticky tape
Scissors

cut slits

2 Fold the card in half along its length. Make small diagonal cuts 5 cm apart along the fold, as shown.

fold into tube shape and tape

3 Open out the card and bend the edges underneath so they overlap. Tape them in place making a long triangular tube.

tape
bend tail down
cut into thin strips

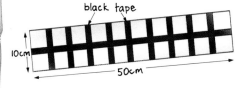
black tape
10cm
50cm

1 Stick black tape down the middle of a piece of thin white card, 50 cm long and 10 cm wide. Criss cross it with black tape, 5 cm apart, like this.

4 Wrap and tape a piece of black paper 30 cm x 25 cm around the last 5 cm of the tail. Cut the end of the paper into thin strips.

Lion and Leopard Tails

Things you need:
Thin yellow card
Yellow crêpe paper and white paper
Sticky tape
Scissors

cut slits

1 Make each tail with a piece of yellow card, about 80 cm x 10 cm, following steps two and three of the zebra tail. Then curve the tubes upwards along the cuts.

tape on tail tuft

2 Make a lion's tail tuft with yellow crêpe paper cut into strips, like this.

tape on white paper tail end
cut slits in tail end

3 For the leopard's tail end, use a piece of white paper, 12 cm by 12 cm. Wrap and tape it around the end of the tail. Cut it into the pointed shape shown. Cut small slits along the bottom edge of the tail end.

Jungle Props

As well as playing tapes of animal or bird sounds, you can beat pots and pans as drums to make jungle music. Serve beasty bites on food frogs and make jungle pots to fill with goodies for your animal friends to take home or to to drink from.

Food Frogs

Turn your paper party plates into funny food frogs. Fold them in half, pinch the corners together and staple them so that they open up like giant frogs' mouths.

Cut out two green, three-toed feet for every frog and tape one foot under each corner. To make eyes, glue small circles on to big green or yellow circles of paper. Tape two eyes to the top of each frog. Use a long, flat piece of carrot as a tongue, or stick on a long, thin curly strip of orange paper.

Jungle Pots

Things you need:
Paper cups
Green crêpe paper and thin card
Sticky tape and scissors

1 Wrap a layer of green crêpe paper twice around a paper cup. Make sure it is wide enough to stick 12 cm above the top of the cup, like this.

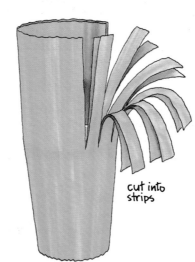

cut into strips

2 Cut the crêpe paper above the cup into a fringe of strips to look like long blades of grass, like this.

ANNA

tape on handle

3 To make a handle, tape each end of a strip of card, about 20 cm long and 3 cm wide, inside the cup. Write one guest's name on each handle. Fill the jungle pots with goodies and give them to your friends to take home.

Use large cups for party pots for your guests to take home their party goodies. Just add straws to small cups without handles as drinking jungle pots.

Monkey Business

Here are three funny jungle games to play with your friends. It is best to get them ready before your party starts. You may need an adult to help you.

Blind Banana Race

Split up your guests into teams of monkeys. Line up a banana for each team at one end of the room or garden. At the other end, blindfold one monkey in each team and spin them around.

The blindfolded monkeys then race to pick up their team's banana and bring it back. Their team members must help them, but only by shouting instructions like, 'forwards', 'left' and 'right'.

Feed the Monkey

Ask two guests to pretend to be baby animals. Put bibs round their necks and sit them on the floor facing each other with their knees almost touching. Make sure their clothes and the floor are covered.

Blindfold each monkey and give them a paper bowl full of wobbly jelly. Then tell the two baby animals to take it in turns to feed each other!

Jungle Noises

This is a game for six people or more. But there must be an even number of players. Before the party, write the name of an animal, such as a lion, monkey, snake and wild pig on a card for every guest. Use an equal number of cards for each animal, say four lion cards, four monkey cards, four snake cards and four wild pig cards (if you have 16 guests). Ask an adult to place the cards in half-hidden spots that are quite easy to find around the room or garden.

Tell the players how many cards there are for each animal and send them off to find one card each. The winners are the ones who find the other players with the same animal cards first.

The fun comes because everyone must do this only by making the sound of the animal on their card.

Beasty Bites

Turn your party table into a jungle with a grassy green cover, leafy netting and salad trees. Get your friends to help you make lots of beasty bite sandwiches and crazy creepy crawlies. Then join them as they munch their way through the jungle to the piranha pond.

Salad Trees

Slice off the ends of a peeled carrot. Cut a notch, about 1 cm deep, in the centre of the thinnest end. Cut more notches lower down on each side.

Stand the carrot in a thick slice of cucumber with its middle cut out to make a tight fit. Wedge a small piece of lettuce into each notch. You can use different kinds of lettuce and different colours to make the leaves.

Banana Birds

Cut a banana in half. Cut a small slit in one side at the top. Push a small thin slice of apple into the slit. Push one or two small ice cream sticks into the end of the banana and freeze it.

Cover the frozen banana with yoghurt and then hundreds and thousands. Freeze the banana again.

Just before serving, cut a black grape in half for the bird's eyes. Push one half on to the end of a cocktail stick. Push the cocktail stick through the bird's head. Break off the end, keeping a little bit sticking out. Push the other grape half on to the end.

Lily Leaves and Floating Flowers

To make a lily leaf, cut a small, thin V-shape from the edge to the centre of a slice of kiwi fruit. For a flower, ask an adult to help you cut a plum into crown-shaped halves. Gently place some leaves and flowers on your jelly pond just before everyone sits down to eat.

Piranha Pond

Things you need:
1 packet of green jelly
Blue and green food colouring
Large foil pie tin
115 g butter icing
Desiccated coconut
Chocolate logs or mini Swiss rolls

1 Make up one packet of green jelly in a bowl or jug. Add a few drops of blue food colouring. Mix it well.

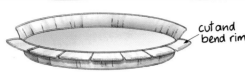

cut and bend rim

2 When it has cooled, pour the jelly into the pie tin and let it set. When it is set, cut around the rim of the tin and bend it back, as shown.

cake board

3 Place a cake board over the tin and carefully flip the jelly over.

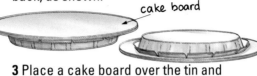

4 Use a hair dryer to warm the bottom of the tin until it can be lifted off completely, leaving the jelly on the cake board.

5 Make the butter icing (see page 11) with green food colouring. Spread it on the cake board around the pond and cover it with green coloured desiccated coconut (see page 24). Position the chocolate logs or rolls and decorate the pond with a frog, lily leaves and floating plum flowers.

Piranhas? Well that's why you should never dip your fingers in the jelly!

Crazy Crawlies

To make bug bodies, cut carrots and cucumbers in half lengthways. Cut two slits in the back of the cucumbers and push half a cucumber slice into each slit.

Push cocktail sticks into the bodies for legs and eyestalks. Push raisins and small pieces of cheese, melon, ham, cucumber and pineapple on to the legs as feet. Add black grape eyes.

Jungle Crush

Cut the top quarter off enough oranges for every guest. Scoop out the flesh into a mixing bowl. Chop it up and take out any big bits of pith. Mix in one spoonful of vanilla ice cream for every orange.

Chill the orange husks and put the mixture in the freezer. When it has turned to slush, spoon it back into the husks. Serve this yummy slushy crush with a straw poked through the top of each orange.

Jungle Cuts

Make lots of tasty sandwiches with white and brown bread. You can choose any filling you want, such as peanut butter, chocolate spread or delicious cream cheese.

Then, using special animal-shaped dough cutters, cut out lots of different sandwich animals. Add raisin or grape eyes. Dot them around your jungle table or put a couple inside each food frog to give to your guests.

EXTRA PARTY PIECES

To help your guests find your house, choose a party prop to hang outside. It could be a pirate's Jolly Roger flag, a fancy royal banner or a bunch of colourful balloons that look like floating planets.

COOKING TIPS

Instead of coconut frosting, make sugar frosting for the rims of glasses. Dip them first in lemon juice, then in icing sugar. Add a few drops of food colouring to the juice just for fun.

To help keep sliced fruit looking nice and fresh, keep it chilled and sprinkle it with lemon juice.

To cover ice cream cones with butter icing, balance each one on the end of a pencil held in one hand. Use your other hand to spread the butter icing with a knife or a spatula.

NAPKIN FLAGS

Turn coloured napkins into party flags. Fold them into triangles over a length of string pinned across the party room.

MOON BALLOONS

Turn plain balloons into floating planets to decorate discos and space parties. Blow up long modelling balloons and tie their ends together to make planet rings. Fit a round balloon tightly inside each ring. Then hang them up by thread from the ceiling or from fences and trees outside.

BEAUTIFUL BADGES

You can easily cover plain badges with pictures cut out of old magazines or books. They could be faces of animals or pop stars, flowers or patterns. It is best to choose a small picture that covers the top of the badge. Cut it out with a little extra all the way around so that you can fold and glue it underneath the badge.

BACKDROPS

Create party backdrops with pictures to suit the party theme you have chosen. Cut them out of old magazines and glue them on to big sheets of paper or fabric. Your friends can have fun seeing how many different animals or pop stars, for example, they can spot and name.

NIFTY PLACE NAMES

You might want to choose who should sit next to you at the top of the party table. Make place names that suit the theme of the party so that everyone knows where to sit. Write on their names in big, bold letters so that there is no confusion.